GAY CAKE

Toho Publishing Chapbook Series I

Sean Hanrahan

TOHO
PUBLISHING

All rights reserved. Published by Toho Publishing LLC, Philadelphia, in 2020.

FIRST EDITION

Cover design by Josh Martin
Cover art/photo by Tanya Kam Hudson (thank you Tanya for an amazing cover!)
Original layout design by Andrés Cruciani

Series editor: Sean Hanrahan

ISBN 978-1-7344992-0-9 (paperback)

"Groom on a Cake" was first published in Stonewall's *Legacy* (Local Gems Press). "Peace in a Church" was first published in *Toho Journal*. "Thoughts on a Gay Suicide, Age 9" was first published in *Mobius: The Journal for Social Change.*

www.tohopub.com

This book is dedicated to all those who know what gay cake tastes like.

"Thoughts on a Gay Suicide, Age 9" is dedicated to the memory of Jamel Myles and his unknowable possibilities. He left us far too soon.

Contents

Marie Antoinette

Let them eat cake 'cept I
can't have any bundled up in
my tumbrel trundling past
doesn't she look fabulous my
pompadour keeps sliding
off my sweaty forehead handing
out petit fours to the
bigots serenading me with
epithet song *faggot*
*cocksucker homo fudg*e packer
chevalier troubadours
of fake rusticity unknown
since Trianon where the
pastoral Ganymedes frolicked
safely under gentle
eaves away from moralizing
eyes on me powderless
brioche stashed in my reticule
oaths made on tennis courts
promise me a speedy trial in
the public opinion
justice system guillotine sharp
rhetorical whetstones
ensures every Robespierre like
an ejaculating
dog has his day when this
country once encompassing
has no place for you and
the sky seemingly limitless
before clouds over with
the miasma of rights denied
to everyone like you

Groom on a Cake

I've decided to take
the plunge off the end of
this cake I am moored in
fondant disinterested
minds conferred whether to
bestow humanity
on us and devised some
greeting card prose legal
meaning we still can't get
married by a preacher
only Cinderella's
fairy godmother with
all the legal standing
such a union implies

We are entitled to
the jokey Bud Lite cans
hitched to Mississippi
mud truck flaps if we crash
the doctors can refuse
us life because of our
rings we both grow dizzy
from the political
whirligig rides that make
us puke cotton candy
on our designer clothes

Separated from my
groom 'cross the vanilla
expanse he loosens his
collar as fiery
judgmental eyes melt him
to a waxen puddle

purple flower submerged
in a supposed sin
I will jump *oh I will
survive* and I will keep
the wilted boutonniere
in anger for remembrance
our assimilation
a miscalculation

Straight Land

I'm the gay one I get fingers snapped in my face.
I'm the gay one my place at the table gets dictated
      by the right, the left.
I'm the gay one I get to hear the hetsplain
      about my pain.
I'm the gay one I get to be rejected by the
      nonconforming and mainstream.
I'm the gay one I get to be the mascot, picture a
      cute dog dyed to match a purse.
I'm the gay one I get to skip church and hate God.
I'm the gay one I get to announce third-party
      politics isn't a box I can check.
I'm the gay one I get to relish the squirms
I cause when I utter the word "sex."
I'm the gay one I get that sixty-nine percent of
      Americans support equality.
I'm the gay one I also get that the thirty-one percent
      oppose the legality of my life.
I'm the gay one I am told I should be judged by
      my character, how refreshing!
I'm the gay one I am told society's getting better
      by those never knowing its oppression,
you know, by those who could pass, those who
      stand for their approbation,
those lucky, manly few who bask in admiration,

      the ones who could ease on over into
      straight land.

Swain Street

Swain Street is it kind of
like Fascination Street
as sung by the Cure for
blonde beaus pulling their pouts
lacy Victorian
dreams when they used to swoon
over a swain Shropshire
lad who just walked in camp
men complaining in a
serpentine Polari
slang they could not have him
migraine tired after
stiff drinks decorating
the corner snug trophies
of misspent afternoons
judging the other poofs
smoke rings telling stories
on the ceiling seen as
continents from the floor
boozy stevedore straights
had no idea what
they were up to rough trade
whistling in the fug
a snifter of brandy
perfumed laudanum sips
chintz on a fainting couch
overdone wallpaper
greeting the boring swain
ungainly stammering
in the parlor looks the
part but somehow he does
not entice or enchant
the cynics of today

America Is the Lie We Tell Ourselves

America is the lie we tell ourselves
to help us rise out of bed each morning.
I wasn't even an American until 2003;
even then my citizenry
was granted provisionally,
subject to the Brooks Brothers vanities
of uncaring politicians.
The hot, stale winds of bigotry
blow from the South, the Midwest,
perhaps from that Indianapolis
Catholic school collecting the names
of LGBT students for *encouragement*.
History and the present teach us
such lists are seldom good ideas.
Perhaps they are building a gay
Noah's ark, and they need two
of every queer. Not a dove, but
a raven will return to herald a renewed
covenant of God's supposed love.

In what ways are we different from
Tanzania or Chechnya? This country
perpetually rounds up the *other*
for a cruelly prolonged sideshow, a Great
Awakening of hate. And in what way,
can we ever become one, not several
Americas? The America of Mississippi
is not the same America as NYC if
you don't conform, if you want to buy
wedding cake, if you read the wrong books,
if you dare attempt to plan a future people don't want
you to have—afraid for their own.
America is that elaborate and beautifully
designed storefront window in which I never

see a place for myself, yet my reflection
always tries to impose itself on the
display. We all memorize the empty
promises of our many anthems and pay
homage to various symbolic state birds. We all
hopscotch over this gerrymandered quilt stitched
with threads of intolerance and pretend commonality.

Masterpiece Theater

I woke up an American, but
I will go to bed a second-class citizen
dreaming of untasted cake.
I wander around dazed by
that untethered feeling
you get when each branch
of the government seeks
to oppress you, silence you, grind you
into the dust in which they think
you came.

I laugh as I shake my fist
at Phillips. He must think bigotry
makes his dick look bigger
as he spins his Burl Ives bullshit
posing as the cuddly bigot
who doesn't hate gays
on the morning tv. My
husband and I clink coffee mugs
to celebrate my fifth decade of being
an *other* in this one nation under
a discriminating god, divisible into so
many slices.

Haphazardly grazing from
Leviticus' banned platter—
showing up to court in his polycotton
blends, snacking on shellfish.
It's petty what passes for sincerely held
religious beliefs. Tell me
did his wife even come
with kine?

Gays get no credit in
the straight world, no
justice under straight law.
We're adjectives lingering
in a dystopian linguistic
conundrum, unwanted,
un-American, cheek stinging
from the uppity faggot
smackdown, but I'm not
into S&M.

We will all be punished
by this straight and
narrow ruling, a detour
back to the '50s, vendors
encouraged to display unwelcoming
signs in their windows. Didn't
Trump promise to make America
straight again?

Conservatives getting hard-ons
watching chyrons dance on
CNN or Fox and Friends—
an endless then forgotten
replay. Pull up a chair,
try to buy a slice of wedding
cake at Masterpiece
Cakeshop. He's just doing
the Lord's work, because
what else did Jesus die
on the cross for if not to discriminate
against gays?

Justice Kennedy thinks
the plodding evangelicals
and the traipsing pansies
need to treat each other
with respect and dignity,
that we should walk off into
a sitcom sunset together
holding hands and singing "Kumbaya"
in a mythical America
that only exists in his mind.
There seems to be this expectation
of incompatibility between homosexuality
and Christianity.

Perhaps, I will renounce cake.
Write a scathing review on his Yelp page
that will disappear before
he can read it. Spend sleepless nights
wondering if this is a turning point
or a small setback. I hate America a bit more
each passing day as I pull crucifix splinters
out of my back and shrug the shredded
remnants of the flag designed
with straight bars and dead stars off my
shrunken shoulders.

Heterosexualize Your Children

Heterosexualize your children.
Homosexual children are *perverted*.

Set them up on dates with children
of the opposite sex. Watch them

pantomime straight wedded bliss.
Call your son a ladies' man.

Laugh when your daughter
wants to marry daddy.

Scream at your children.
if your son dares to become

a gentleman's man,
or if daughter wants to marry mommy.

Then you absolutely must shame them
into heteronormativity.

Push them into a corner
where the straight lines intersect

other proper straight lines.
Lock them in their rooms.

Tear down their same-sex crush posters.
Disable their search egines.

Remove all joy from their existence.
Kick them out of the house.

It's ok if neglect and spanking do not
achieve the desired results.

Remember, gay conversion therapists have
the right voltage to fix your children,

the praying influencers, the programmable guilt.
You can even rewire your adult children,

especially in New York!
Coercion works at any age.

Just the other day, it was my honor
to overhear a five-year-old boy

say to two men who had the gall to get married,
"Two married men, that's silly."

How great he has learned that so young!
We have taught our children well.

In childish hate, there is great wisdom.

Earning Your Keep
Inspired by Clueless

Cake boy to all who know
except blondes blinded by
lust white sock footsie on
a frilled canopy bed
he loves Tony Curtis
in *Spartacus* biceps
secreting oil from the
steam bath desiring the
spunky taste of oysters
spouting '50s lingo
dancing with the muscly
'til dawn what's his favorite
flavor does he approve
of funfetti frosting or
the mid-nineties frosted
tips of a current ska
band leader dresses well
but cake boy is left out
of candids the wallet
bound group shots respected
but feared good for a laugh
but never let into
the circle of jerks who
quote Jim Carrey like he
quotes Shakespeare acceptance
reached only if you can
teach them all the mating
gyrations and scold them
about dialing down the
Drakkar and matching ties

Peace in a Church

I.

Atheist I pace the contours of a grandiose church
just as I lazily trace the body of my lover
on those rare Sundays where we can lie in late
because no one, certainly no god, needs us
for a while, on those days when the world
has forgotten us, and we couldn't
        be more grateful.

II.

Gothic Europe seems to have transported itself
smack dab in the middle of North Carolina,
a time machine gone awry, pomp smothered
in hominy, twangy hallelujahs custom-designed
to awaken Jesus. A strange, mystic, incensed
Catholicism wafts through this avowedly Methodist
        church.

III.

Bishops and slave owners stand guard over
the entrance. Goodly men laboriously defended
at every turn, no matter the evil they harbored,
ignored, or fought for. Not seeking a history lesson,
or erasure, I enter the suddenly quiet space as if the
building has some medieval power to shut the world
        out.

IV.

Waiting for the prognosis, Mom anesthetized
and face-down on a strange bed in a beige and sterile
operating theater, and all my husband and I can do
is wander and take in this anomalous architecture
and scrutinize the transponder as if we were waiting
for a table at one of the numerous chain restaurants
       that encircled my youth.

V.

There is peace in a church, no solace perhaps,
no coloring book Jesus to rest his hand on my
shoulder with encouraging clichés and tantalizing
tautologies, but a respectful silence missing in
the hospital waiting room where Fox News pundits
battle reruns of where-the-hell-did-you-dredge-
those-up '70s TV shows that demonically torment my
       eardrums.

VI.

In fact, the only people who disturb me are the few
shutterbugs mindlessly snapping away at this
opulence, trusting in their phones and not their
minds to remember, not welcoming the blurry,
rain-damaged ends of a memory that I prefer
or the ideas that a place provokes instead of
a simply factual, poorly framed
       reality.

VII.

It is time to face the news without a heavenly support system, or a choir of angels with magical, acapella band-aids for your soul, just our concern for my mother, and the few minutes of peace I found in a place I least expected. The stained glass winks at me as I walk out into the suddenly, oppressively hot southern summer air.

Explosion

It's a good day to be gay.
Don't feel so alone
among the S&M crowd—
the standers and the modelers—
I overhear that pre-Stonewall joke.
The afternoon smells like a perpetually lit cigarette
that may be due to the recent refinery explosion
or the dwindling cutoff-clad smokers behind me.
I don't even begrudge the straight couples
holding hands and walking slow,
which they can do anytime, anywhere,
not only during festival season.
We can be gay but briefly in the age of MAGA.
No slurs today yelled from tall figures
or tinted windows.
Mayor Pete is a long shot for the presidential nom,
but it's a good day to be gay.
The gym queens with their guns out—
those sculpted pink pistols—
kiss kiss on the sidewalk
before taking a communal shower.
Pride flags, unburnt, unfurl in the June heat.
Pride displays in chain store windows create
a queer Christmas for those who believe.
It's that rare perfect day to be gay
when bigotry and violence are erased
from the final draft.

Sensitive Issue

Snacking on a melted
TastyKake watching the evening
news—a soothing bedtime
story about homophobic
Christian missionaries
(American, of course!)
flocking to Uganda to preach
the Elmer Fudd gospel
of *kill the faggot* enshrine it
in law Leviticus
whoever the fuck he is nods
his approval from an
Old Testament heaven where gays
cannot enter and the
anchorman with Malibu Ken
hair concludes the piece with
sage words of how important it
is to hear both sides of
this sensitive issue moral
relativism has
now broadened to include murder
unprovoked thunderbolts
from Discrimination Jesus
the only one I know
the only one who grows here in
American soil just
add clumps of processed sugar from
thoughtless minds—the Twinkie
defense (ask Dan White)—and droplets
of Anita's orange
juice the deity invoked in
mass media consumed by good-
hearted people code for bigots

gays hold church of their own
sharing brunch with straight refugees
from other religions
that accept them but I digress
clinking mimosas since
the last time we attended Mass
we heard *take of this cake*
and eat it except you faggot
nobody died for your sins

The Moroccan
Inspired by the Henri Matisse painting

I learned the gourds were not
other heads bowed down
in prayer and that you were alone
among the flowerpot and the minaret.
I didn't know one could pray out of belief
and not for show. How different you seem
from my own compatriots
who would usurp this Matisse
with their artful piety—
heads erect not bowed,
Jesus or the Holy Spirit glistening
from their conditioned roots to their
designer sneaks. I understand you, solitary
worshipper, although I don't comprehend,
nay suffer from, monotheism,
no place for gays like me in it,
so I reject it. Yet, somehow,
I intuit you wouldn't reject me.
You are painted too beautifully,
too truthfully. The brushstrokes that
comprise you suggest a heaven I have
not been sold before. You take me out
of this crowded museum space
and into your peaceful cubist world.
You beckon me to join you on the prayer
rug—a communion in the casbah without
the sickeningly sweet wine. For once, I
can lose myself in the contemplation of
God, if only for a few hazy moments
until someone jolts me or another
painting not as serene catches my eye.

Bird and Butterfly

I cradle a bird and butterfly bowl in my sun-warmed palm, captured to a near eternity in ceramic glaze. Both the animals and the stoneware technique can flit across the arbitrary international border.

In the emporium on Avenida Revolución, Raul, an elderly Mexican gentleman spry in the way non-Americans are spry, explains to me the origin of Tonala pottery. In the 1950s, a tourist from Kansas City fell in love with the fragile art painted on burnished clay and shared his knowledge of stoneware with the local artisans to make their art last longer. They formed a group named El Palomar (dovecote) and continue to honor him in their work today.

Raul continues to tell me the stories concerning all the pieces I trace with inquisitive fingertips as a common theme of American and Mexican unity emerges. Our conversation blossoms to encompass his life in Tijuana, recently relegated to most-dangerous-city-in-the-world status. But Tijuana denizens can go to church, school, celebrations without worrying about gun violence.

He made his children watch American television to learn English. He expresses concern over how the media portrays his city, how the US government vilifies Mexico. He makes a veiled reference to the wall, an unnecessary construction consuming us all. And here I am, on a trip of pique, a trip of atonement, wishing I could resurrect my high-school Spanish. I want to buy something from every store. I want my American dollars to float from till to till in another country.

I mention to him the woman I met crossing the border so she can afford a crown, result of the non-affordable health care acts. I try to express to him that borders unfortunately have power, but they do not really have meaning.

I buy the bird and butterfly to remember him, so one day I can remember the fleeting beauty of butterflies and Tijuana. I buy the bird and butterfly to celebrate the forgotten fact that the world is full of kind stories and strangers.

If you don't know where to find them, they are usually hanging around the art.

Rainbow Capitalism: A Pantoum

Now that we've embraced rainbow capitalism,
perhaps chain stores will fly Pride colors,
since our govt. sure as hell won't.
The sartorial binaries are stocked and loaded.

Perhaps chain stores will fly Pride colors.
We fought back, we resisted.
The sartorial binaries are stocked and loaded,
we still have to perform hetero norms for the masses.

We fought back, we resisted.
We paraded down city streets in jacked-up heels,
we still have to perform hetero norms for the masses.
Do we owe everyone our assuredness and sass?

We parade down city streets in jacked-up heels,
since our govt. sure as hell won't.
Do we owe everyone our assuredness and sass,
now that we've embraced rainbow capitalism?

Image to Flatter

I.

Two ordinary men trapped in daguerreotype
for a perpetual near eternity,
    a slow filmic erasure framed by hazy foliage.
Dotted eyes earnest for adventure
    whether they be soldiers, friends, brothers,
lovers jutting elbows
    playfully jostling to gain supremacy.

II.

I rescued you both,
if you want to call it that,
    from an art fair in the northwest part of town
where you were congealing
    to other dusty, forgotten lives.
No family to reclaim you.
    Maybe, your photograph was a discard,
since neither of you are centered,
    and a fraction of a top hat is left to the side.

III.

Your story reminds me of one I cannot recall,
    so I bought you a shiny frame with
    professional backing
to document this secret escapade
    or disappearance into a big city.
Both of you eager to know
    love that was proscribed, the positions
my blasé companions and I take for granted.
    To reflect my history, I hung you, handsome
        gentlemen,
as if you were my friends.

IV.

Your blank stares suggest you seek to escape
        my prearranged conjecture,
my anachronistic claim you are gay men,
        my fictional ancestors.
My real ones were buried with their proclivities.
        Please forgive me, there are so few portraits
to guide me in how to be
        in an era that demands constant
        shapeshifting.
I have many roles to inhabit.
        There are many images to flatter
before the last shutter.

Stonewall Transcendence
Dedicated to the Pulse nightclub victims

They prettied the park to commemorate Stonewall
codifying rebellion into federal property
where defiant bricks once found copper heads
where steep stilettoes once dented chrome.

Alabaster statues now stand celebrating love captured
in surreal photographs by hurried tourists or gauzily
veiled in salty tears by the pilgrims
who never thought this moment—a recognition
beyond ourselves—would arrive.

I once got robbed around here after leaving the
duplex—a trick gone sinister—
few would believe such a crime could happen now
with the squadron of police cars
and counter-terrorism experts willing
there not to be another Orlando.

Not many can recall when the only law enforcement
who cared about the safety of gays
were the Guardian Angels
or the Christopher Street Patrol.

Trouble now comes from bridge and tunnel invaders
grasping at hate to replace the emptiness
of their souls littered with 7-11s and
punning church signs just by-products
of an unimaginative suburban wasteland,
sacrificial lambs on the altar of anomie.

Standing still
standing proud
standing silent
I watch flowers bloom in a park
that hasn't seen them in nearly
one hundred years of progress.

A shiver runs through me
as I reflect that a gay pilgrimage site
has been made sacrosanct
by the same government that thirty years ago
ignored us thus marking a generation for early deaths
when unwritten sonnets littered the Village streets
like invisible un-mourned funeral wreaths.

This moment this split second of transcendence
gives me hope some small sense
that one of the stars or the stripes
on the American flag fluttering
in this holy queer space
may represent *all of us*.

Adam Rippon

Skate grace you've had hardships
sissy on the flipside
of society's dream
flaunt sparkled shirts flawless
triple axels precise
hands express lifetimes spent
on the margins bounded
by potential violence
if the femme obvious
slips through the hips at the
wrong time being told you're
not ok don't wear that
don't talk that way lisping
is gay friends taken from
you the bad influence
you're queer contagion and
no parent wants fey for
a child skate proud more of
a representation
a moment just for us
than America a
nation wary of our
difference our flamboyance

Really Good Guys

Not invited 'round for
birthday cake with blue confetti
sprinkles 'cause parents thought
our lisping was too sinister
less apple pie and more
tarte tatin teachers stuck to their
lesson plans while we were
bullied on the playground taunts of
gay girl sissy left to
whimper in the back of class told
insults build character
faggot keyed into our lockers
our hearts our minds our souls
*I'm gonna jump that Catholic school
faggot* sick days became
respites childish threats morphed into
drunken frat boys yelling
*I'm gonna kill that faggot Nah
he's not worth it* should we
be glad that our lives are spared or
saddened to learn our lives
are worthless but they are *really
good guys* these white straight men
who tell us what is good enough
for us what rights we should
have tell us where we can buy cake

Thoughts on a Gay Suicide, Age 9
Dedicated to Jamel Myles

Were we nine the first time
someone called us faggot
gay homo queer too femme
for school? Did our classmates
have the epithets then?
Could we understand what
they meant, cower from their
power? Could they smell it
on us? Or hear it in
the melody of our
voices? See it in the
way we threw a baseball?
Did we stare too long at
the other boys, crushes
killed before they could start?
We knew the words to all
of Madonna's songs, and
we could sing them in tune.

Torn between cartoons and
the worldliness that was
thrust upon us. Trusted
around china since we
were gentle. Invited
to tea parties where we
combed ratty unkempt hair
of neglected Barbies.
We had to listen to
problems because children,
even adults, thought we were wise,
preternatural when
we were just trying to
drown in appropriate

boy concerns, but others
locked the gate to us so
Bugs Bunny style we dug
underneath convention
and tried lipstick for Fudd.
Each day, innocently,
we drew a line between
us and them, deepening
during puberty. Lives
shrunk to a muttered word.

At fourteen, a good day
involved not being called
faggot, which always sounded
like *ribbit* in the croaked
voice of a surly teen,
scrawniness covered in
sweats and Starter jackets,
puffing out unformed chests
always about to jump
us but scared under the
front. By eighteen, we cared
less or endured more. Hate
was internalized not
as common but present
when guys smirked under trees
as we walked by alone,
minds so alert to threats,
we could never daydream.

Could we have been saved by
a butch jock stance as our
fathers thought sport stats would
make the other boys warm
to us? No room for the
theatrical ones in

the '80s. Had to learn
to unlike the girl things,
throw out Miss Piggy and
fancy stickers, claim our
favorite book was *Tom
Sawyer* not *Wizard of
Oz*. Tried to be manly,
but the growth spurts never
came so we stayed slender,
small targets in size eights.

Bullies can follow us
into the bedroom now,
screens not streets away. It
took only four days to
kill Jamel age nine who
learned how cruel the world is
early when he still liked
sugary cereal,
drew shaky figures in
crayon with an untrained
hand, was still under five
feet tall. We are told it
gets better, but where is
the proof. Policies shield
schools from consequences
as a child is hounded
to death. We ask you to
imagine yourself at
nine. Was suicidal
ideation even
a possibility?

If so, this poem is
dedicated to you.

About the Poet

Sean Hanrahan is a Philadelphian poet originally hailing from Dale City, Virginia. He is the author of *Hardened Eyes on the Scan*, published in 2018 by Moonstone Press. His work has also been included in several anthologies, including the *Moonstone Featured Poets, Queer Around the World,* and *Stonewall's Legacy.* His work has been published in several journals, including *Impossible Archetype, Mobius, Peculiar, Poetica Review,* and *Voicemail Poems.* He currently serves on the Moonstone Press Editorial Board, as head poetry editor for *Toho Journal,* and as an instructor for Green Street Poetry. Stay tuned for his first full-length poetry collection, *Safer Behind Popcorn,* coming from Cajun Mutt Press in early 2020.

www.ingramcontent.com/pod-product-compliance
Lightning Source LLC
Chambersburg PA
CBHW031635040426
42452CB00007B/846